FIRST
PEOPLES
of NORTH
AMERICA

THE PEOPLE AND CULTURE OF THE
SHOSHONE

CASSIE M. LAWTON
RAYMOND BIAL

Cavendish
Square
New York

Published in 2017 by Cavendish Square Publishing, LLC
243 5th Avenue, Suite 136, New York, NY 10016

Library of Congress Cataloging-in-Publication Data

Names: Lawton, Cassie M., author. | Bial, Raymond, author.
Title: The people and culture of the Shoshone / Cassie M. Lawton and Raymond Bial.
Description: New York: Cavendish Square Pub., [2017] | Series: First Peoples of North America | Includes bibliographical
references and index. | Description based on print version record and CIP data provided by publisher; resource not
viewed. Identifiers: LCCN 2015045348 (print) | LCCN 2015044796 (ebook) | ISBN 9781502618979 (ebook) |
ISBN 9781502618962 (library bound) Subjects: LCSH: Shoshoni Indians--History--Juvenile literature. | Shoshoni Indians-
-Social life and customs--Juvenile literature. Classification: LCC E99.S4 (print) | LCC E99.S4 L38 2016 (ebook) |
DDC 978.004/974574--dc23 LC record available at http://lccn.loc.gov/2015045348

Editorial Director: David McNamara
Editor: Kristen Susienka
Copy Editor: Rebecca Rohan
Art Director: Jeffrey Talbot
Designer: Amy Greenan
Production Assistant: Karol Szymczuk
Photo Research: J8 Media

Printed in the United States of America

ACKNOWLEDGMENTS

The People and Culture of the Shoshone would not have been possible without the kind help of several organizations and individuals who have committed themselves to preserving the traditional ways of the Shoshone. We are especially indebted to the men and women who helped secure photos, as well as to Cavendish Square Publishing for making this book possible. As always, we offer our deepest affection our families and friends who have encouraged us along this journey.

CONTENTS

A Shoshone woman dresses in traditional clothing.

AUTHORS' NOTE

At the dawn of the twentieth century, Native Americans were thought to be a vanishing race. However, despite four hundred years of warfare, deprivation, and disease, Native Americans have persevered. Countless thousands have lost their lives, but over the course of this century and the last, the populations of Native tribes have grown tremendously. Even as America's First Peoples struggle to adapt to modern Western life, they have also kept the flame of their traditions alive—the languages, religions, stories, and the everyday ways of life. An exhilarating renaissance in Native American culture is now sweeping the continent from coast to coast.

The First Peoples of North America books depict the social and cultural life of the major nations, from the early history of Native peoples in North America to their present-day struggles for survival and dignity. Historical and contemporary photographs of traditional subjects, as well as period illustrations, are blended throughout each book so that readers may gain a sense of family life in a tipi, a hogan, or a longhouse.

No single book can comprehensively portray the intricate and varied lifeways of an entire tribe, or nation. We only hope that young people will come away with a deeper appreciation for the rich tapestry of Native American culture—both then and now—and a keen desire to learn more about these first Americans.

The landscape of the Shoshone territory includes towering cliffs and gently flowing rivers, such as the Snake River, shown here.

CHAPTER ONE

The Shoshone were also called Snake people by other Native tribes and early explorers.

A CULTURE BEGINS

Many thousands of years ago, the first Native Americans entered North America by way of the **Bering Strait**. These men, women, and children formed family groups and dispersed throughout the continent, eventually forming civilizations. Each community had its own language, beliefs, and customs. One of these groups formed into the Shoshone (shuh-SHO-nee) Native American tribe. This group of people had a major impact on early European explorers—particularly after President Thomas Jefferson made the **Louisiana Purchase** in 1803. One of the most famous Native American women in US history, Sacagawea, came from the Shoshone tribe. This is the story of the Shoshone's culture and their people.

Becoming the Shoshone

The Shoshone have traditionally lived in a vast region known as the **Great Basin**, located between the Sierra Nevada and the Rocky Mountains. Stretching from the desert country of eastern Oregon to northern Arizona and New Mexico, the Great Basin encompasses nearly all of Nevada and half of Utah, most of western Colorado, parts of Idaho and Wyoming, and a portion of eastern California. The Shoshone shared these lands with other Native peoples, notably the **Bannock**, Paiute, and Ute, with whom they intermarried and shared many customs.

The ancestors of the people living in the Great Basin arrived in the region some time between two thousand and one thousand years ago. Originally, they spoke a language called **Numic** (NUH-mik). In time, the ancestral language developed into several closely related modern languages, including Northern Paiute, Ute, and Shoshone. These Numic languages, as they are called, belong to the Uto-Aztecan language family. Users of these languages lived everywhere from Central America to Oregon and include not only the Numic group but Hopi and Aztec, among others.

Over time, the people of the Great Basin split into three separate groups: the Northern Paiute,

Other areas of Shoshone territory had vast expanses of brush and mountains.

the Southern Paiute, and the Shoshone. The name Shoshone (also spelled Shoshoni) may derive from the Native word *sonippeh*, meaning "high-growing grass," or possibly "valley dwellers," although the origin of the name is uncertain. The name may also come from a different Native word, *shoshoko*, meaning "walkers," a reference to the Western Shoshone, who did not have horses. The Shoshone refer to themselves as *niwi* (NUH-wuh) or *nimi* (NUH-muh), meaning "person," and *niwini*, meaning "people." Other tribes referred to them as "Snake," possibly because some Shoshone groups lived near the Snake River. The first English accounts from Meriwether Lewis and William Clark refer to the "Sosones [Shoshone] or snake Indians."

The Shoshone gradually drifted into three groups: the Western Shoshone, the Northern Shoshone, and the Eastern Shoshone. The Shoshone bands came together for **tribal councils**, bison (also called buffalo) hunts, and other major events. When they did so, the Shoshone did not consider themselves to be separate bands. A nomadic people, the Shoshone migrated to wherever game or edible plants could be found. The Northern Shoshone and the Eastern Shoshone became skilled horsemen and buffalo hunters.

The Western Shoshone roamed central and northern Nevada, western Idaho, and northwestern Utah, as well as the Panamint and Death Valleys in California. Several tribes made up the Western Shoshone, including the Gosiute (or Goshute), Cumumbah, Tosawi, and Koso (or Panamint). Because much of their territory was desert, life was especially challenging for the Western Shoshone. Struggling to find enough food and water for their own survival, they had little opportunity to develop a complex society. They lived in small bands, which came together about once a year. They traveled by foot and relied on dogs as beasts of burden, even after horses had been introduced to the Great Basin in the seventeenth century. There was simply not enough grass in their territory for the grazing of horses. The Western Shoshone survived primarily on seeds and plants. They occasionally ate a little meat obtained from hunting and fishing. Their religious ceremonies were based on the Round Dance, and they acquired supernatural power through dreams and visions.

The other Shoshone shared similar languages and some customs but otherwise lived quite differently from the Western Shoshone. The Northern Shoshone lived in eastern Idaho, northern Utah, western Montana, and eastern Oregon. They were divided into bands:

Western Band (including the Wararereeka), Mountain Band (including the Lemhi), Northwestern Band, and the Pohogwe Band (or Fort Hall tribe). The bands tended to gather in large villages for long periods of time. Over time, the eastern bands of Northern Shoshone began to ride horses and hunt bison like Native peoples on the **Great Plains**. The Northern Shoshone also began to fish for salmon—a skill they learned from the Nez Perce, who lived nearby in the northern Plateau country. Like the Nez Perce, the Northern Shoshone also gathered the bulbs of a lily known as **camas**. Dried and stored, camas bulbs were an essential source of food during the winter. Unlike the Western Shoshone, the Northern Shoshone lived in large villages, headed by strong chiefs. These chiefs led hunting and fishing expeditions and made alliances with other tribes.

The Eastern (or Wind River) Shoshone made their home in western Wyoming. They later became known informally as Washakie's Band, in honor of their greatest chief. Early in their history, the Eastern Shoshone ventured out to hunt on the Great Plains as far north as present-day Canada. Like the northern plains tribes, they rode horses, hunted bison, and went to war in large, well-organized groups. Under the authority of a strong central leader, the Eastern Shoshone were the most strongly unified of all the Shoshone groups. During the winter, they scattered into small family groups and camped in valleys sheltered from the wind and snow. They remained in the valleys where there was enough grass for their small herds of horses until spring, when they came together again. In the late autumn, under the leadership of a great chief such as Washakie, they came together again and hunted bison.

After the Northern and Eastern Shoshone acquired horses in the late 1700s, they gradually extended their bison hunting to the east. However, they increasingly came into conflict with the Plains tribes, notably the Blackfeet and the Arapaho. In 1782, a smallpox epidemic devastated the Shoshone, and they were not able to withstand the assaults of their Plains rivals, especially after the Blackfeet acquired firearms. Later, the Northern and Eastern Shoshone were driven back to their original territory in the Great Basin by the Sioux and the Cheyenne, who were themselves being pushed westward by settlers.

The Europeans and then the Americans became another source of pressure. The Shoshone first encountered people of European descent in the early 1800s, when a young Shoshone woman named Sacagawea guided the Lewis and Clark expedition to her homeland. Over the next several decades, the Shoshone attempted to relate peacefully with trappers and traders. However, the settling of the Mormons in the Great Basin in 1847, the discovery of gold in California in 1849, and the opening of the Oregon Trail brought a seemingly endless flow of settlers through their homeland—and rapid, wrenching changes for the Shoshone. Although the Shoshone often allied with US Army soldiers, serving as scouts and warriors, they at times also fought against these troops. By the late 1800s, the Shoshone were forced to abandon their homeland and move onto **reservations**.

Adapting to the Land

Hot, dry, and rugged, the Great Basin is one of the harshest areas in North America, yet the Shoshone adapted and learned to survive there. The Sierra Nevada and Cascade Mountain ranges block the moist air sweeping in from the Pacific Ocean. As the air rises over the mountains, the moisture is released as rain or snow on the western slopes. However, the rain shadow—the eastern side of the mountains and the rest of the Great Basin—receives very little precipitation. On some barren peaks there is not enough rain for any plants to grow, while other mountains support only scattered grasses and a few meager trees. In some places, however, there is often enough spring runoff to fill ponds and streams with ice cold water. During their autumn dances, in the hope of receiving enough water, the Eastern Shoshone used to sing, "Send rain on the mountains! Send rain on the mountains!"

Much of this sandy, rock-strewn landscape alternates between mountains and valleys—with especially lofty peaks and broad valleys in the northern and eastern parts. Throughout the region, even on the flattest stretches of land, mountains are always seen poking up through the distant haze. The changes in elevation determine the climate on the mountain slopes. Toward the tops of the slopes, the air becomes markedly colder, and there is usually a little more rain and snow. On the valley floors, bristly cactus, succulents, and several kinds of yucca thrive in the dry soil.

There is great variety in the desert landscape. Warm deserts, such as the Mojave in southern Nevada and

California, are dominated by creosote bushes. The cold deserts of the north are covered mostly with sagebrush and saltbush. Sagebrush and grasses also flourish on the lower slopes of mountains in the southern parts of the region. At higher elevations, there are forests of juniper and **piñon** and stands of scrub oak, ponderosa pine, aspen, spruce, and fir. In the north, the vegetation changes from sagebrush to juniper and piñon, followed by another layer of sagebrush and grasses, then forests of conifers. In the far north, brush and grasses dominate the valleys, with forests of Douglas fir, ponderosa pine, spruce, and other large trees at the higher elevations. Above the timberline, a few small plants grow in the south, while lovely flowers cling to the craggy peaks in the northern reaches of Shoshone territory.

Along with the mountains and valleys, there are canyons and plains. In the central and southern parts of the Great Basin, the Colorado River has carved dramatic canyons with towering walls of layered rock. By contrast, in the north, there are plains of deep soil and lush grasses between the streams that flow into the Green and Snake Rivers. The region is also dotted with spring-fed marshes. Fish, frogs, and turtles flourish on this moist, spongy ground of cattails and bulrushes.

Otherwise, the arid land is better suited for scaly lizards, slithery snakes, and rodents and birds that have adapted to the dry climate. In the true desert, the burrowing rodents include kangaroo rats and pocket mice. Horned larks, vesper sparrows, and western kingbirds glide through the air, while jackrabbits and kit foxes, symbols of the desert, venture from their underground burrows. Other rodents like woodrats and

The Shoshone hunted bison, also called buffalo, for their food and clothing.

ground squirrels live in the sagebrush and piñon trees at the fringes of the desert, as do cottontails.

The Western Shoshone caught many of these hardy creatures and used them for food. They also hunted the pronghorn antelope and the buffalo that occasionally wandered into their territory, and in the winter they stalked the mule deer that descended the slopes in search of better grazing. In the mountains, bighorn sheep and elk grazed, and the Shoshone pursued them as well. Red squirrels, porcupine, marmots, and beavers were also often added to the cooking pot. The

Shoshone shared the hunting grounds of the Great Basin with mountain lions, wolves, foxes, and hawks. Coyotes also wandered throughout the deserts and mountains, feeding on any small creature that came their way. Salmon migrated seasonally to the rivers that laced the northern parts of the Great Basin. Trout and other fish abounded in the lakes and streams.

Through each of the four seasons, Shoshone bands came to know this territory as they hunted, fished, and gathered seeds and berries. Over the generations, they learned much about the plants and animals that provided them with food, clothing, shelter, tools, and medicine. They came to understand the climate and territory in which they lived. Without this knowledge, the Shoshone would never have survived on the often-harsh land where they had made their home.

Storytellers of the West

Like many tribes in the American West, the Shoshone told stories to pass time and to pass down knowledge and understanding about the world around them, their beliefs, and their traditions. Many of these stories involved the characters Coyote and Wolf. Both a trickster and a provider, Coyote was also the creator of the Shoshone people, as related in the following story from the Western Shoshone:

> One day, Coyote was walking through the mountains when he met a pretty young woman. She was carrying a jug of water. He approached her and said, "I am very thirsty. Please give me a drink of water."

She pointed to a place about a half-mile away and told him to meet her there and she would give him a drink. Coyote did so and asked, "Is this the place?"

"No, it is farther," she told him.

She went ahead, and when Coyote caught up with her, she again told him, "No, it is farther."

In this way, she managed to trick him repeatedly until she reached her home.

The girl lived with her mother, who asked, "Where did you get him?"

"He followed me," the girl answered in dismay.

Coyote began to drink some of the water.

"Stop that!" the young woman cried, repeatedly striking at him.

However, Coyote dodged each of the blows as he drank his fill. The young woman then told him to go into the lodge. Inside, Coyote noticed many bows and arrows in the quivers hanging on the walls. He suspected that these were the weapons of other warriors who had visited the mother and daughter and been killed by them.

Coyote was afraid of the beautiful young woman, but he was also very much attracted to her. That night the mother told him, "You go and make a bed outside."

Reluctantly, Coyote went to sleep on the ground outside the lodge. In the morning, the old woman said to him, "There are many arrows in the lodge. Take them and a bow. Hunt all day and kill many ducks."

Coyote did as she requested and returned with many ducks. The old woman plucked the birds and cooked them. They had a great feast that night. Thereafter, Coyote stayed with the women and went hunting every day. He was in love with the young woman, and they got married.

As the days passed, the old woman made a very large water jug. She carefully wove the basket and coated the inside with pitch so that it would hold water. When the basket was finished, the old woman told Coyote, "You must go home now. Carry this jug with you."

Coyote was very puzzled. Why must I now leave, Coyote wondered, and why does she want me to take this jug? But he knew that he should ask no questions.

The old woman added one last instruction, "Do not open the water jug during your journey. Do not open it anywhere. When you come to the middle of the country, you may then open the jug."

Overcome with curiosity, Coyote now wondered what could be inside the jug. However, instead of asking any questions, he simply did as he was told. Saying goodbye to his wife and her mother, he started his journey, carrying the jug, which was very heavy. What can be in this jug, he wondered.

The Shoshone were connected to the land.

Why is it so heavy? Coyote remembered the old woman's warning not to open the jug, but he was so curious.

One little peek will not hurt, he told himself. With a rock, he hammered at the plug wedged into the neck of the jug. As soon as he pulled out the stopper, young men and women jumped out. They were all fine-looking people. As he continued on his journey, the inquisitive Coyote opened the jug again and again. Each time people sprang from the opening. Who are these people, he asked himself.

As he came to the end of the journey, Coyote realized that the people were the children from his marriage with the young woman. And this is how the Shoshone and the other Native people came to live in many small bands throughout the Great Basin.

Over time, the Shoshone adopted Western ways of dress. Here Chief Tindoor and his wife pose for a picture, circa 1850s.

LEMHI CHIEF TINDOOR

CHAPTER TWO

[Shoshone women] collect the wild fruits ... attend to the horses ... cook ... and make all the apparel ... in short the man does little.

—Lewis and Clark

BUILDING A CIVILIZATION

The Shoshone were not like other Native groups. Their communities developed over time, but some bands became meshed with other Native groups. Many Shoshone lived nomadic lifestyles, choosing to travel during different parts of each season. Some Shoshone did join together to form the bands known today, complete with their own leaders, beliefs, and traditions. Each member would play a role in making his or her community a thriving place to live.

Shoshone Life

Shoshone people originally lived in family groups dispersed throughout the West. During the winter, Western Shoshone families came together in small villages named for a nearby landmark or a particular food that was gathered there. Although they lived together during this time, the families were so loosely united that none of these camps could be considered a band. Related by blood and marriage, the families shared customs. However, chiefs or headmen had little authority over the group other than to oversee hunting or gathering activities.

The leaders of Northern Shoshone bands changed frequently, and people often moved from one group to another. Some bands, especially those that lived in the west, did not even have a chief. However, those in the east, such as the bands living around the Snake and Lemhi Rivers, often had to join together to embark on large-scale bison hunts and to defend against enemy attacks. The bands also united for councils and feasts, which were led by a principal chief and several other headmen. These positions were not hereditary and changed often. Band councils also arose to restrict the authority of chiefs. Groups of warriors formed soldier societies, which may have also kept order during important gatherings such as bison hunts and dances.

Over the course of the eighteenth and nineteenth centuries, the Eastern Shoshone became the most organized of the three branches of the Shoshone—especially when the bands came together for the bison hunt in the spring and the Sun Dance in the summer.

They also strongly united under a central leader when they battled the Blackfeet, Arapaho, and other tribes of the Great Plains.

Holding the most vital position in the band, the chief had to have a range of exceptional abilities. He had to be wise and experienced, at least middle-aged, and have the proven skills of a warrior and the training of a medicine man. The chief was responsible for major decisions, especially those regarding hunting, migration, and warfare. Along with his assistants, he had authority over two soldier societies. He also served as diplomat in any conflicts with other tribes. To signify his elevated status, he lived in a **tipi** (TEE-pee) painted with specific designs and wore an elaborate headdress.

During the winter, the Eastern Shoshone separated into three to five bands and camped in the Wind River valley. Each band had its own chief and soldier societies to help maintain order. Families were not required to stay with their own band. They often joined other groups for the winter. Some even settled with other tribes, such as the Crow.

Dwellings

The Western Shoshone built cone-shaped huts, even in the winter. Those who lived in the mountains covered their huts with bark mats or brush. To protect themselves from the intense sun, the Western Shoshone built shades. To make a shade, they lashed together a framework of branches and covered it with brush. They sometimes placed brush in a circle to break the wind and provide a little shade. Some families, however, did not put up any kind of dwelling. When the weather got bad, they took shelter in a cave.

The Shoshone built tipis in which they lived and hosted ceremonies throughout the year.

Tipis

When the Northern and Eastern Shoshone lived in the Great Basin, like many of the Western Shoshone, they made cone-shaped homes out of wooden poles covered with sagebrush, grass, or woven willow branches. As bands gradually migrated eastward onto the Great Plains to hunt bison, they began to live in tipis, which were better suited to a nomadic way of life. They covered their tipis with woven rushes and willows and eventually with buffalo hides, like the tipis of the Sioux, Cheyenne, and other Plains tribes.

Made of long, slender lodgepoles and stitched bison hides, a tipi could be easily set up, taken down, and hauled to the next camp. To put up a tipi, several women lashed three or four poles together and raised them, spreading out the bottom ends so the frame stood upright. To complete the tipi, they filled in the sides with ten or more smaller poles and wrapped a bison-hide cover around the cone-shaped structure.

Making a cover required hours of labor. Women first spread fresh bison hides on the ground and scraped away the fat and flesh with bone or antler blades. They next dried the hides in the sun and scraped off the coarse brown hair. After soaking the hides in water for several days, they rubbed them with a mixture of animal fat, brains, and liver to soften them. After rinsing the hides in water, they smoked them over a fire to give them a tan color. Several women then laid out several tanned hides and carefully stitched them together.

The covering was attached to a pole and raised and then wrapped around the frame. Held together with wooden pins, it had two wing-shaped flaps turned back at the top to form a vent, or smoke hole. These flaps could be closed to keep out the rain. Another flap, which covered the U-shaped doorway, could also be closed. Men often decorated their tipis. Inside, the spare furnishings included beds, a fireplace, and leather pouches called **parfleches** (par-FLESH-es) in which food was stored.

During a heat wave, the bottom edges of the tipi were raised so the wind could circulate through the dwelling. In winter, people often built a berm, or sloped earthen wall, around the tipi for better insulation. They also hung a dew cloth made of bison hides on the inside walls from about shoulder height down to the ground. Decorated with paintings of battles or

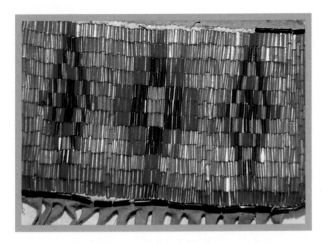

The Shoshone made jewelry using minerals and beads.

dreams and visions, the dew cloth kept out dampness and created pockets of insulating air. With a fire burning in the center of the earthen floor and bison robes for bedding, tipis remained warm even during the coldest months.

Working together, several women could quickly and easily take down a tipi. They folded the covering and used two of the tipi poles as a **travois** (trav-OY), a kind of V-shaped sled, to carry the covering, poles, and their belongings to the next camp. The poles were strapped to a horse and the ends dragged on the ground. A travois proved to work even better than a wheeled cart on the bumpy ground.

Using the Bison

During a spring hunt, the Shoshone could obtain enough bison meat to feed themselves for months, along with an abundance of hides and bones for making tipis and tools. Because the Shoshone moved so often, household goods had to be light and durable. Pottery could be broken on their long journeys, so they stored food, clothing, and other belongings in parfleches and baskets.

Although the Shoshone had to journey great distances in search of the herds, the abundance of meat that could be found made these migrations worthwhile. The band might camp near the herd for several weeks, usually along a stream fringed with trees, where they had a good supply of fresh water and wood. Often at war with the plains tribes, the Shoshone picked campsites that could be best defended from attack.

The Shoshone created many works of art, including baskets in which to carry items such as berries and water.

The Importance of Horses

The Eastern Shoshone and Northern Shoshone prized their horses. Ever since Spanish mustangs entered the wild, horses had populated the Western United States. For the Shoshone and other Native tribes, horses helped carry people and goods, as well as made wide-ranging expeditions for hunting, trading, and warfare possible. Horses were never eaten, unless the band faced starvation. Hides and bones were never made into tools or household goods, although horsehair was an important fiber. A horse that had been wounded in battle was decorated with paint and feathers. Owners attentively brushed their valuable mounts. When a man died, his favorite horse was often ritually sacrificed at his grave. It was believed that horses had spiritual powers and could predict one's future. For instance, if a horse pawed rapidly three times, making a row of half-moon marks on the ground, it was believed that the owner would soon die.

The Eastern Shoshone owned many horses, and men, women, and children were highly skilled riders. Men usually cared for the warhorses, while women managed those horses used as pack animals. Men and women each had different saddles. Men used a pad thrown over the back of the horse, while women preferred a Spanish-style saddle with a high pommel, cantle, and stirrups. These saddles were often elaborately adorned with beadwork. Other riding gear included halters, bits, reins, lassoes, and rawhide whips.

The Shoshone—especially the Eastern Shoshone—became experts at raising and training horses as both riding mounts and pack animals. Male horses were gelded, or neutered, so they would be gentle. Men taught riding horses to move at several speeds, or gaits. Some riding horses were specially trained for

Once introduced to the Shoshone, horses became very important parts of Shoshone life.

the dangerous work of pursuing bison. These bison horses had to respond to the rider's knees so he had free use of his hands to shoot arrows or thrust a lance into his quarry. Packhorses, however, were taught only to walk and trot. The horse became a highly valued and essential resource on the long, dry stretches of the Great Basin and Plains.

Nomads Join Forces

As nomads traveling the land, some bands of the Shoshone lived independently, while others chose to unify with other Native groups to form a more diverse and stronger unit. The Northern Shoshone were one such group. They traveled together for many years over the landscapes of Idaho, following large migrating game such as bison. In the 1600s, they joined with the Northern Paiute, or Bannock, tribe. The Bannock had originated in Nevada and Utah, but in the seventeenth century, they moved onto land in present-day Idaho. The Bannock sought to join forces with the Northern Shoshone living there, particularly for hunting bison. Over the years, the two tribes continued to travel and hunt together. They had similar languages and customs, but their tribal practices were kept separate. Eventually, the tribes would be forced onto reserved land in Idaho, becoming the Shoshone-Bannock Tribe known today.

The Shoshone, as a people, mastered many skills that they passed on to other generations. By the time they encountered the first Europeans, the Shoshone bands had established themselves as some of the main forces in the West. Their determination helped them survive many hardships and continue thriving in the present day.

The People and Culture of the Shoshone

The Shoshone decorated themselves and their horses in beads, feathers, and leather fringes.

Since the earliest instances of the Shoshone, elders have passed down Shoshone stories and traditions to younger generations.

CHAPTER THREE

There, in a distant place, she sits in an arroyo, winnowing the pine nuts. By the red-rock-wooded place, winnowing the pine nuts.

—Western Shoshone song

LIFE IN THE SHOSHONE NATION

The Shoshone practiced many beliefs, customs, and traditions. Many events were the result of a key moment of life, such as birth, maturity, and death. Among the Shoshone groups there were many different traditions. Not all of them were shared by each Shoshone band. However, despite differences, all of the Shoshone valued family life and the importance of celebrating life's many stages.

Life Cycle Traditions

The Shoshone celebrated many of life's events. They had different practices for the birth of a baby, for ensuring a child's growth, and for bidding loved ones farewell. These are some of the rites once observed by several Shoshone groups.

Being Born

When a woman was about to give birth, she retired to the menstrual lodge. An older woman would serve as midwife during labor. The mother remained in the lodge for up to thirty days. Her husband observed certain prohibitions during this time. For instance, he did not eat meat, and he did not visit his wife or the baby for fear that he might bleed to death from the nose. A messenger told him of the birth, and later when the umbilical cord had fallen off, he was allowed to eat meat again.

Among the Western Shoshone, parents did not eat grease or meat after the birth of a baby. They were not allowed to touch their babies' heads, which were considered the source of the strength and wisdom that was to be imparted to the infant. A female baby was especially welcomed because she would someday attract a mate who would help the family in its continual search for food.

Growing Up

Shoshone parents rarely punished their children. Usually, a gentle scolding was all that was required to remind children that they were expected to be

A Shoshone mother carries her child in a cradleboard.

cooperative for the good of the group. The Western Shoshone sometimes sang a song to warn their children that Wolf might snatch them if they misbehaved:

Furry Wolf,
On his back he carries him away,
Carries him away,
Carries him away,
Upon his tail he carries the child away.

From an early age, boys and girls helped the adult women gather berries, seeds, and nuts. Children also raided birds' nests for eggs. In preparation for communal hunts, children helped to gather the brush used to build the corrals into which the jackrabbits and other small game would be driven. With bows and arrows, boys learned to hunt squirrels, which were gladly added to the cooking pot. With a pair of stones, girls ground pine nuts from piñon trees into a coarse meal.

Children also enjoyed a number of games that helped them learn the many skills they would need as adults. Northern and Eastern Shoshone children staged

Shoshone tribes had many rituals for their children, which changed slightly as the generations progressed. Here, Shoshone children gather for a photo at the Wind River reservation, circa 1947.

The People and Culture of the Shoshone

mock battles and bison hunts. In these imaginary hunts, one boy would bellow like a bull bison, and the others would pursue him. Children also played hoop-and-stick, a test of skill in which they guided a hoop over the uneven ground with a stick. Children shot arrows at targets and competed in footraces to develop the endurance they would need to survive the rigors of life in the Great Basin. Children also played a game similar to cat's cradle with a piece of string made from sagebrush bark. Using their imaginations, they always had plenty to do in the plains and desert around them.

Maturing

When a Western Shoshone girl had her first menstrual period, she was isolated in a separate hut and had to observe certain restrictions. She was not allowed to eat meat, for example, or carry firewood. The Western Shoshone required girls to remain in brush huts as a coming-of-age ritual. However, afterward, women did not have to live apart whenever they had their period. Among the Northern Shoshone, the opposite was true—every woman retired to the menstrual lodge when she had her period, but there was no puberty ceremony. Afterward, a girl was given new clothes, and her body was painted to show that she had become a woman and was now ready to be married.

Like the girls, boys also had to follow certain rules. A boy was not allowed to eat the first game he killed, so that he would learn a lesson in abstinence. As he approached adolescence, a Shoshone boy went on a **vision quest**. Leaving camp, he journeyed alone into the hills to seek a sign or message from the spirits.

Early Shoshone people created rock art. Here is a Shoshone pictograph showing a shaman with powers.

These spirits would help him to become a skilled hunter so that he might support his family, and a great warrior so that he might defend his people. The spirits not only gave him power but guided him for the rest of his life.

Marrying

Girls helped their mothers until they married, which usually occurred not long after puberty. A suitable husband had to be a good provider. Often, he was a somewhat older man who had already proven his skills as a hunter. The Shoshone did not have formal courtship and wedding ceremonies. Marriages happened in one of three ways:

1. A union could be arranged by the girl's parents. They chose a mate for her and usually offered the young man gifts to induce him to marry her.
2. A man could also simply stay with a young woman. He might live in her lodge for about a year or until their first child was born. Or, if she agreed, he might take her to his camp where they would begin to live together.
3. If a man saw a woman he liked, even if she was already married, he could capture her, often fighting her husband for her. In this case, the woman unfortunately had no say in the matter. However, she could later return to her family if she wished.

Dying

The Northern Shoshone and the Eastern Shoshone wrapped their dead in blankets and placed the bodies in rock crevices where wild animals could not reach them. Mourners cut their hair and sometimes gashed their legs. They destroyed the dead person's horse, tipi, and other property in a sacrificial ritual. They believed that the soul of the departed journeyed to the land of Coyote or Wolf, who were revered as great spirits among all the Shoshone.

The Western Shoshone buried their dead in caves or cremated the bodies, often burning the remains along with the home of the deceased. Mourners cut their hair, and spouses waited at least a year before they married again. It was believed that the ghosts of the dead could be very dangerous. Even dreaming about the deceased could bring misfortune. While in mourning, the Western Shoshone did not eat grease or meat. They were also not supposed to wash during this time. After a year of mourning, a ceremony was held in which a leader symbolically washed away the mourners' grief. Objects that had not been buried with the body were also burned in a sacrificial fire.

War Practices

Warriors equipped themselves with shields, lances, war clubs, and bows and arrows. The Sioux referred to the Shoshone as the "Big Shields." Before they adopted horses, warriors fought behind large round shields that completely protected them. Made of bison hide, the shields were covered with painted buckskin. As they faced the enemy, the warriors stood close together so the shields touched, forming a wall. To further protect themselves, warriors put on sleeveless tunics made of six layers of antelope hide. With a mixture of sand and glue quilted between the layers, the armor could not be pierced by arrows. However, the tunics could not stop bullets, and as guns spread across the plains, the Shoshone abandoned this form of armor.

The Eastern Shoshone were continually at war with other tribes from the beginning of the eighteenth century until they moved onto their reservation in 1868. They fought the Blackfeet and later the Arapaho, Sioux, Cheyenne, and Gros Ventre. During the late 1800s, they came to rely on the US Army as their main ally. Warriors organized around two soldier societies: the Yellow

Many Shoshone men participated in war parties.

Brows and the Logs. With up to 150 courageous young warriors, the Yellow Brows served as the vanguard, leading the way during migrations. They also kept order during bison hunts. When engaged in battle, they fought to the death. Made up of older men, the Logs guarded the rear of the band during marches. Members of both societies went to war in the spring and especially the fall. Warriors who proved themselves in battle were entitled to paint black and red finger marks on their tipis. Warriors were also entitled to blacken their faces in preparation for battle.

The Northern Shoshone traditionally fought the Blackfeet and the Nez Perce. Their weapons included bows made of cedar or the horns of elk or mountain sheep, along with poison-tipped arrows kept in otter-skin quivers. They chipped obsidian into sharp arrowheads and knife blades. In close fighting, they wielded stone war clubs. Antelope-skin armor and bison-skin shields offered some protection during battle. After acquiring horses in the 1700s, the Northern Shoshone adopted many of the war customs of the plains tribes, such as taking scalps and "**counting coup**." Warriors counted coup by approaching an enemy close enough to actually touch him. To shoot an enemy from a distance did not require as much courage as riding or running up to him. Warriors also counted coup by stealing horses and undertaking other acts of bravery. The Shoshone adopted the Scalp Dance, in which warriors celebrated their victorious raids and battles, from the plains tribes.

The Western Shoshone historically fought the Utes. However, they had to devote so much time and energy to eking out a meager existence that they seldom went to war with other groups.

Hunting

Like the tribes of the Great Plains, the Eastern and Northern Shoshone came to rely on the bison as their primary source of food. The Eastern Shoshone went on a bison hunt in the spring. This was followed in early summer by a Sun Dance, their most important annual ceremony. In the early autumn, they often joined the Bannock and the Flathead tribes for a large communal hunt. In later years, they often traded hides and dried meat from these hunts for horses, pack animals, and European goods.

Once a grazing herd had been located, young men rode out to it on horseback. Galloping alongside the beasts, these daring hunters shot arrows or thrust lances deep into the heaving chests of the bison. After the hunt, the women quickly butchered the carcasses where they lay scattered over the plains. Hunters had rights to the animals they had killed, but everyone who participated in the hunt received a share of the meat. The liver and other organs that quickly spoiled in the heat were cooked and eaten right away. The tongue, hump meat, and ribs, considered to be the choicest parts of the bison, were also cooked and eaten at the scene of the hunt.

Most of the fresh meat was loaded on travois and hauled back to camp. There, women sliced the meat into thin strips and hung it on wooden racks to dry in the sun. Sometimes, they built fires under the racks to keep flies away and quicken the drying time. Women pounded some of the dried meat, called jerky, into a fine meal and mixed it with berries to make **pemmican**. People sometimes ate pemmican as a snack, but most often men used it as energy food on long journeys. Most of the dried meat, however, was stored for the winter months ahead.

Gathering and Fishing

After the spring bison hunt, Eastern Shoshone women gathered fruits, berries, roots, and wild plants—notably camas, wild onions, and sunflower seeds—for the rest of the summer. Men caught fish—mostly cutthroat trout, Montana grayling, and Rocky Mountain whitefish— especially in the early spring when supplies of food were low. They made **weirs**, or traps, by placing rocks or brush across a stream, leaving a narrow opening through which the fish were forced to swim. Sometimes, they placed a willow basket across the opening to scoop up the fish more easily. The fish were eaten fresh or dried in the sun or smoked over a low fire for later use.

Next to bison and fish, elk was the most important source of food for the Eastern Shoshone. The men either ran down entire herds or tracked single animals. They also hunted mule deer, antelope, moose, bears, and mountain sheep. Jackrabbits, beavers, and other small game, as well as ducks and other birds, supplemented their diet. In the autumn, the Eastern Shoshone embarked on another hunt after the bison had fattened on summer grass. Through the long and lean winter months, they sustained themselves largely on dried bison meat.

Northern Shoshone men also not only pursued bison on horseback but hunted mountain sheep, deer, elk, and other large game. Disguised in antelope skins, a hunter often crept up on an animal or, riding a horse, ran down an antelope. People also caught fish, including trout, perch, and sturgeon, but mostly salmon, in the rivers that laced through their territory. Standing on platforms or wading into the water, men speared or netted the fish. They also built salmon weirs across streams. With sharpened, fire-hardened sticks, women dug prairie turnips, tobacco root, bitterroot, and especially yampa root and camas bulbs. The roots were either boiled or steamed for several days in pits dug in the ground. Hot rocks were placed in these earthen ovens along with the roots, then the pit was covered with soil. The women also gathered seeds and berries, especially chokecherries and serviceberries. Some Northern Shoshone also gathered pine nuts.

Animals such as elk were vital to the Shoshone way of life.

Throughout the spring, summer, and autumn, the Western Shoshone walked to the places they knew abounded with edible plants and animals. However, game was scarce in the desert, and the Western Shoshone ate much less meat than the other tribes. Women picked greens in the spring and gathered many kinds of grasses, along with seeds, berries, pine nuts, and roots, through the summer and autumn. They made these seeds and roots into cakes. With digging sticks, they harvested wild turnips and other roots, which they then baked in pits beneath hot rocks until soft and brown. With beating sticks, women knocked seeds loose, or they collected seed heads, which they tied into bunches. Small seeds and pine nuts were carried in baskets. In areas where piñon trees were abundant, the Shoshone depended on the pine nut harvest. The Panamint and Death Valley Shoshone also ate mesquite pods. They ground the pods between two

RECIPE

BISON STEW

Here's a modern recipe for the traditional favorite food of the bison-hunting Shoshone:

INGREDIENTS

2 pounds bison meat cut into 1-inch (2.54-centimeter) cubes

4 medium potatoes, peeled and cut into 1-inch
  (2.54 cm) cubes

6 carrots, peeled and sliced

2 onions, chopped

2 stalks of celery, cut into 1-inch (2.54 cm) pieces

1 16-ounce (473-milliliter) can stewed tomatoes

2 6-oz. (177 mL) cans of tomato paste

2 tablespoons (30 mL) vegetable oil

1 teaspoon (5 g) marjoram

1 tsp. (5 g) thyme

2 cloves garlic, minced

1 bay leaf

2 tbsp. (30 mL) Worcestershire sauce

¼ tsp. (1.25 g) pepper

½ tsp. (1.5 g) salt

¼ cup (32 g) flour

about 2½ cups (591 mL) water

Place the vegetable oil in large kettle or Dutch oven and brown the meat (about 3 minutes). Add onions and sauté until translucent. Add about ½ cup water (enough water to cover meat), tomato paste, and seasonings. Cover and cook one hour over very low heat, or until meat is tender. Add potatoes, carrots, celery, stewed tomatoes, and additional water to cover. Cover and cook ½ hour over very low heat or until vegetables are tender.

Remove meat and vegetables. Thoroughly mix ¼ cup flour with 1 cup water. Add slowly to the hot broth, stirring continuously. Place meat and vegetables back in gravy and reheat.

The stew is now ready to serve.

stones and shaped the flour into cakes that were easily stored. In the desert country, people also sustained themselves on salvia seeds, cactus, agave, and gourds. Seeds were threshed and ground, then boiled, roasted, or stored for later use.

Although most of the Western Shoshone's food came from plants, men provided some meat for their families by hunting game, especially bighorn sheep and antelope and sometimes deer. Men either ambushed the bighorn sheep or stalked them. Antelope were driven into a V-shaped corral made of brush or stones where they were easily shot with arrows. Rabbits were another major source of meat. Often, the entire band joined in a communal hunt in which they drove jackrabbits into nets made of twisted grass twine. They trapped cottontails in deadfalls and snares. The Western Shoshone dug out burrowing rodents, especially pocket gophers and ground squirrels, with sticks. They also flooded or smoked the rodents out of their holes. The Western Shoshone occasionally caught fish in streams. They also hunted birds, including doves, quail, sage hens, and ducks. In some regions, people sustained themselves on grasshoppers, crickets, and insect larvae. During the winter, several families settled in camps near their caches of dried meat, pine nuts, seeds, and other foods.

Clothes and Accessories

Shoshone clothing varied according to how close the bands lived to the plains and its huge herds of bison. The Shoshone inhabiting the eastern and northern parts of the Great Basin made their clothes from bison hides and occasionally the skins of elk and other big game. They often fringed their shirts along the seams and decorated them with quillwork bands on the shoulders. Made of elk skin, the leggings often had fringes. The Eastern Shoshone decorated their clothing more elaborately than either the Northern or Western Shoshone, most often with buckskin fringes, quillwork, and, later, glass beads. They were especially fond of blue-gray beads.

During warm weather, Shoshone men usually wore only a breechcloth of animal skin, fur, or bark fiber. It was drawn between the legs and tied around the waist. As winter approached, men donned leggings and long shirts that hung to their thighs. Shirts were made from the hides of bison, deer, antelope, bighorn sheep, or occasionally elk. If skins were not available, women wove strips of sagebrush or juniper bark into leggings for the men.

During the summer, women wore a front apron made of animal skins or woven fibers, such as sagebrush or juniper bark. Sometimes, they also wore a back apron. As the weather became cool, they put on leggings similar to those worn by the men and long dresses made of animal skins or woven fibers. With sleeves reaching to the elbows and hems extending to the calves, the dresses were tied at the waist and decorated with feathers, hooves, bird claws, or elk teeth. Later, Shoshone women adorned their dresses with beads and patches of red cloth obtained through trade. In the nineteenth century, many women began to wear European-style dresses, but others—especially the Western Shoshone—continued to wear the

This man wears traditional Shoshone garb, including an eagle headdress.

traditional garments of the Great Basin until well into the twentieth century.

For much of the year, men, women, and children went barefoot. During cold weather or times of travel, however, they put on **moccasins** made from deer, elk, or bison hide. Shoshone moccasins had rawhide soles and seams stitched along the outer edge. Moccasins for winter use were made from animal skins with the hair left on and facing inward. For greater warmth, these moccasins were also stuffed with fur or grass. Sometimes, people wore moccasins of woven sagebrush bark. In the late 1800s, women began to favor high-top moccasins decorated with beadwork. These moccasins were similar to the footwear of the other plains tribes.

People often wore robes, usually made from rabbit skins. To make a robe, strips of rabbit fur were woven or whole pelts were sewn together. Sometimes, women made robes from the pelts of beaver, marmots, and other small animals. During the coldest weather, they bundled themselves in thick robes made from deer, antelope, or bighorn sheep hides, or they kept warm in thick bison robes. The Western Shoshone usually had only robes made from rabbit skins or woven sagebrush bark. However, this style changed over time. By 1900, most people were wrapping themselves in mill-made wool blankets decorated with Native American designs instead of animal-skin robes.

Traditionally, Western Shoshone women in California wore round basketry hats, while those living closer to the Basin favored a taller basketry hat. Other Western Shoshone women preferred helmet-like hats of woven sagebrush bark or willow. Men usually did not wear anything on their heads, but by the mid-nineteenth century, many had adopted feathered warbonnets like those worn by men of the plains tribes. With beaded headbands and a crown of eagle feathers, these ornate headdresses were worn on special occasions.

Both men and women sometimes wore belts made from strips of fur or leather. They also carried buckskin pouches and bags, which were often painted with geometric designs. Sometimes they wore bands of fur

These moccasins show the Shoshone Rose.

or iron, called armlets, on their upper arms. Lewis and Clark noted that the Shoshone also wore collars made of twisted sweetgrass decorated with porcupine quills, shells, or elk teeth.

Both men and women wore earrings and many necklaces. Beads made from small animal bones or teeth—especially elk teeth—were most favored in making jewelry. Sometimes, the claws of brown bears were strung with the beads. Both men and women pierced their ears, from which they hung strings of beads or pieces of abalone shells. Lewis and Clark also noticed that the Shoshone liked to wear metal jewelry, including pewter buttons, earrings of copper and brass, and bracelets of iron, tin, copper, and brass. Some men and women had tattoos on their faces, arms, and legs. Women were often tattooed on their chins. On special occasions, the Shoshone also painted their faces with designs of wavy lines and horseshoes, along with figures of snakes and bears.

As cloth became available, the Shoshone made dresses, shirts, and other clothing from calico, broadcloth, and other fabrics. By the early twentieth century, most people were wearing store-bought clothes. Women preferred long skirts or dresses, along with cotton scarves and fringed shawls. Many men began to wear tall black or white felt hats. As many of the old ways were being transformed or forgotten, the Shoshone no longer saw the need to dress in the same manner as their ancestors. However, by the early 1900s, a number of individuals had begun to revive the old styles. They refined their artistry, especially in creating elaborate beadwork designs on clothing. Among the best-known examples of distinctive artwork are soft-soled moccasins with floral beadwork in a pattern that has come to be known as the Shoshone Rose.

Arts and Crafts

The Shoshone produced handicrafts that helped them survive in an often-harsh environment. They used materials from plants and animals to make tools, weapons, household utensils, and other everyday objects that were both practical and beautiful. The Eastern and Northern Shoshone depended primarily on the bison as a source of raw materials for their handicrafts. Like the Sioux and Cheyenne, the Shoshone began to record the history of their people on elk and bison hide paintings. Having become accomplished horsemen, they also came to make and value elaborately adorned saddles, halters, and whips.

In addition to the meat, the Shoshone made good use of virtually every part of the bison, including the hide, hooves, and bones. Stiff rawhide was stretched to cover drums and war shields. Rawhide strips could be braided into tough ropes, and sinew was used as sewing thread. Scraped to resemble white parchment, skins were folded and stitched together to make parfleches for belongings. The Shoshone frequently painted their parfleches and other rawhide goods with geometric designs, especially rectangles, triangles, and diamonds. They also decorated rawhide with beadwork in geometric patterns. The women tanned the tough hides into supple buckskin to make tipi covers, robes, blankets, clothing, and moccasins. Men fashioned tools—knives, scrapers, and needles—from the bones. Horns were softened and shaped into spoons, cups, and ladles. The hooves were made into rattles. Even the tail could be used as a flyswatter. For the Shoshone, a single bison provided the materials for most of their tools and household objects. They also burned dried bison chips, or manure, as a fuel for their fires.

The Western Shoshone wove useful objects from grasses, willows, and other plant materials. All the people of the Great Basin twisted plant fibers into nets for catching fish in rivers and rabbits in the brush. However, Shoshone women were best known for their basketry. They turned willow branches, sagebrush bark, and other fibers into dishes, trays, bowls, cups, and ladles, and many kinds of baskets used for gathering, carrying, winnowing, storing, and cooking. A basket was often sealed with a coating of pitch on the inside to make it watertight. Because water was often scarce, especially in the desert country where the Western Shoshone lived, it was essential to carefully store this vital resource.

The Shoshone also made use of many kinds of stones. They carved soapstone into pipe bowls and small dishes. They chipped other easily flaked stones— usually flint, obsidian, or slate—to make knife blades and points for arrows and spears, as well as scrapers, chisels, and other tools. With glue and sinew, they attached these sharp points onto feathered wooden shafts to make arrows. They often strengthened the wooden shafts of their bows by applying sinew onto the back. Arrows, along with a fire drill used for kindling fires while on a journey, were carried in an otter-skin quiver. Later, they traded for iron, which gradually replaced their stone weapons and tools.

The various branches of the Shoshone developed skills in many areas, creating unique crafts, clothing, and weapons to accompany their many traditions. Some of these examples of artwork and craftsmanship survive in museums or with current members of the Shoshone tribes today. Many customs adopted by the early Shoshone people are no longer practiced, however. Nevertheless, the Shoshone uphold the history of their people and continue to celebrate many ancient customs today.

Many Western Shoshone considered Appe, the Father and the sun god, to be the creator of heaven and Earth.

[The Shoshone] believe that the sun is a gift from God, our Father above, to enlighten the world.

—Dick Washakie, son of Washakie, a Shoshone chief, in the late 1800s

BELIEFS OF THE SHOSHONE

Like all Native American tribes, the Shoshone had their own religious beliefs and practices. Each band had different rituals and traditions to accompany certain beliefs. As the years progressed and European settlers arrived in Shoshone territory, some Native people grew to accept different religions. Today, some Shoshone bands still practice the traditions of their ancestors.

Many rituals took place in a sweat lodge, pictured here alongside Shoshone men.

Early Religious Beliefs

There were different ideas as to who created the world
in which the Shoshone lived. Many Western Shoshone
revered the sun, which they called **Appe**, or Father.
Some said he had created heaven and Earth. Others
believed that Coyote had created the world, while some
Northern Shoshone held that Wolf was the creator. The
Northern Shoshone and Eastern Shoshone adopted
the vision quest along with other beliefs and rituals of
the plains tribes. The Eastern Shoshone and Northern
Shoshone sought the help of good spirits through
dreams, visions, and journeys to sacred places. It was
believed that these guardian spirits could heal illnesses,
shield warriors from flying arrows, and bring misfortune
to one's enemies. The spirits also told people how to use
medicines to tap their own personal powers. People also

refrained from eating certain foods and avoided various practices that were considered **taboo**.

The Shoshone believed that some people, places, objects, and activities had sacred powers—for good or evil. They feared ghosts and whirlwinds, both of which could bring misfortune. It was believed that sickness and death came from evil spirits or breaking a taboo. The Shoshone revered certain objects, such as eagle feathers and paints. They also honored certain activities, such as smoking wild tobacco and burning sacred grasses Ritual sweating in **sweat lodges** was also a popular spiritual activity. There, they called to the spirits to help in healing themselves.

Treating Illnesses

Most illnesses were treated with herbs, charms, and sweat baths. However, the Shoshone also had medicine men and women, who were specialists in healing. Among the Northern Shoshone, medicine men were especially skilled in the use of roots and herbs for treating injuries such as cuts and bruises. They also invoked charms and relied heavily on the sweat lodge in curing many ailments. Shoshone medicine men obtained their spiritual powers through visions during a fast on an isolated mountain peak or other sacred place. It was believed that Western Shoshone medicine men could also capture the souls of antelope so the fleet-footed animals would be easily guided into corrals.

Rituals and Celebrations

All three Shoshone tribes held seasonal ceremonies with much dancing and feasting. The Northern Shoshone held a special rite, the Round Dance, especially when the salmon returned in the spring, when seeds and nuts were harvested in the autumn, and during times of hardship. The Western Shoshone also held Round Dances during rainmaking and courtship rites, as well as during times of plenty. The Eastern Shoshone, in particular, held many celebrations, notably the Sun Dance and the *naraya*, or Shuffling Dance.

This is a scene from a Sun Dance at the Fort Hall Reservation.

The Sun Dance

Adopted from the plains tribes around 1800, the Sun Dance involved fasting and thirsting. It was a time dedicated to visionary experiences and has been described as an occasion of sacred joy.

Held over several days and nights during the summer, the Sun Dance symbolized the strength and unity of the Shoshone as a people. Within a circle of twelve poles, men danced around a central pole topped with a bison head and an eagle. The men's chests were pierced with sharp sticks and tied to rawhide thongs, which were attached to the sacred pole. Tied to the pole, the men danced for hours without water and endured intense pain.

At the end of the dance, the men tore themselves free, the sticks and thongs ripping through their flesh. They took part in the Sun Dance to prove their courage and endurance but did not undergo the hardship for personal glory. Instead, they hoped that their sacrifice would bring cures and other benefits to their band. Today, the Sun Dance remains an important aspect of some Native American cultures; however, the piercing aspect is only practiced by a few communities.

The Shuffling Dance

The Shuffling Dance was a kind of Round Dance in which the participants slowly moved in a circle, stepping with one foot then dragging the other foot to meet it—to the accompaniment of song. The two main purposes of the Shuffling Dance were to prevent disease and to renew the earth so that plants would give abundant fruit.

Other Native Religions

Since about 1900, many Shoshone—especially the Eastern Shoshone—have been drawn to the Peyote religion. Originating among Native peoples of Mexico and the American Southwest, this religion joins ancient Native American beliefs with Christian elements. They believed that the use of peyote, a hallucinogenic obtained from a cactus plant, helped them to better relate with the supernatural world and renew their

The peyote plant.

own spiritual powers. They also believed in a singular deity, which conversed with their followers through spirits. This religion spread across the United States in the late nineteenth and early twentieth centuries. As they endured painful hardships, many Shoshone found meaning, direction, and hope in this religion. Today it is also known as the Native American Church. More than fifty tribes in the United States and Canada believe in the faith.

With the rise of European settlers in the area in the nineteenth and twentieth centuries, the message of Christianity was preached to the Native American population. Missionaries such as the Mormons brought their beliefs to the Shoshone and other tribes and converted many to their religion. Today, many Shoshone are Christians. However, others continue to devoutly practice their traditional beliefs, including participation in intertribal Sun Dances.

Fun and Games

The Shoshone played a variety of games, ranging from juggling stones to jacks. Games were not only a form of entertainment but a means of achieving wealth through gambling and status within the group. The hand game was popular among the Shoshone and other Native

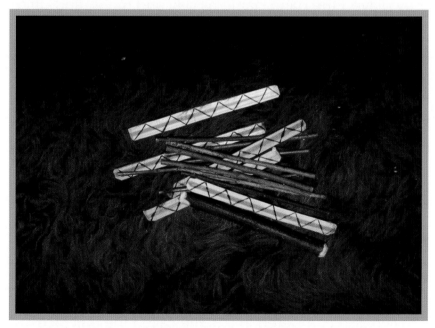

Kids and adults enjoyed playing games, such as sticks.

peoples in the Great Basin region. Sitting on their heels in two rows, two groups of people faced each other from opposite sides of a log. Any number of men could take part in this hotly contested game, but each side had one leader. The contestants used ten small bones as playing pieces and sticks as counters to keep score. One set of bones was plain, and the other was marked with a black strip. The leader handed the bones to his players as they sang songs and beat the log with sticks. The players shuffled the pieces and hid them in their hands. The leader of the opposing players tried to guess who was holding the bones. If he guessed correctly, his side gained possession of the bones. If he was wrong, his side lost a counting stick. The side that had to give up all its counting sticks lost the game. People often became so carried away in a contest that they played the hand game all day and night, and often there was heavy betting on the outcome. The high stakes included horses, bison robes, and hides.

People of all ages, including men and women, also liked a game played with four sticks made from split willows painted red on their rounded sides. A scoreboard made of rawhide was placed in the center. People guessed and gambled on what number of each side would turn up with each throw of the sticks. The Shoshone also bet on footraces that were run over great distances, often by pairs of young men. During the summer months, when camped in the mountains, Eastern Shoshone bands often competed in games and races with the Bannock and other tribes.

Men also competed in a game called the ball race in which opposing teams kicked a stuffed leather ball across a goal line. Women often played shinny or double-ball shinny, a game similar to modern-day field hockey. Teams with five to ten people each met on a field about 75 yards (68.5 m) long. Double-ball shinny was played with two buckskin balls that had been tied together. Each player had a stick and tried to toss or carry the balls over the opposing team's goal line. In shinny, players used a single buckskin ball about 3 inches (7.62 cm) in diameter and advanced it down the field with J-shaped sticks. A team had to score only once to win the game, but this was so difficult that it might take all afternoon to get the ball over the goal line.

Pastimes

People also liked to come together to listen to stories, especially during the long winter nights. Both entertaining and educational, these stories recounted the origin of people and the relationships among various animals. Here is one story from the Western Shoshone about how ingenious Coyote brought fire to the world:

> At one time, all the birds and animals were like people and lived with them. But there was no fire in the land where they lived. One day, as Lizard was lying in the sun to keep warm, he noticed a strange object floating lightly down from the sky.
> Rushing over, the people asked, "What is it?"
> Coyote told them, "It is an ash from a fire in another country. Someone must fly high into the sky to find that place."

Many Shoshone wore animal skins to channel the power of the animal.

"I can go," said Hummingbird, and the little bird flew into the sky and looked in all four directions. After gazing toward the west for a long time, Hummingbird flew back to the people.

Everyone gathered around him. Coyote asked, "What did you see?"

Hummingbird replied, "There is a great body of water to the west. On its shore, many people are dancing around a great fire."

Coyote suggested, "We must go there and get that fire."

So, the people journeyed west. Coyote stationed some of the people at intervals along the way. As he and the other people approached the fire, Coyote disguised himself with a wig made from string. He then joined the people and danced. Luckily, they did not notice that he was a stranger. All through the night, Coyote tried to catch a little fire with his false hair as he danced with the people. Near morning, he at last caught the fire in his hair and ran away.

Shocked that they had suddenly lost their fire, the dancers raced after Coyote.

Coyote hurried to the first man he had posted and gave the fire to him. This man ran to the next man. In this way, the fire was relayed along the route until it came to Jackrabbit, who placed the fire on his tail and sprinted away. Jackrabbit's tail was blackened by the fire—as it is to this day.

Rat waited in his house burrow on top of a rock high on a cliff. As Jackrabbit sped toward Rat, the pursuers caused hail to fall from the sky. Some of the hailstones struck Jackrabbit, who squealed in pain as he scampered along the path. Hearing the cry, Rat scurried down the cliff. He took the fire from Jackrabbit just as the pursuers caught up. Eluding the pursuers, Rat scrambled to the entry to his house. He held the fire close, and it burned a red mark on his chest that he bears to this day.

Slipping into his burrow, Rat placed the fire in a large pile of brush. No one could ascend the cliff, so Rat and the fire were safely hidden in the burrow. But no one had fire now. Below the cliff, the people begged Rat, "Please give us some fire."

So, Rat flung the brush in all four directions and the people hurried to get a bit of fire. Finally, everyone had fire—and the brush still holds the fire. One can simply take a stick from the brush and use it as a drill for making fire. This is how Coyote and the other animals brought fire to the people.

Many of the Shoshone's customs and beliefs have continued to the present day, including some of the ceremonies first enacted by the original Shoshone tribes. Present-day men and women of the Shoshone bands keep their history and traditions alive each year by performing ceremonies such as powwows and sweat ceremonies. As long as new generations are learning about their heritage, the practices of the first Shoshone will continue into the future.

A ground-blessing ceremony for the Sacagawea Interpretive Center.

Beliefs of the Shoshone

Sacagawea (*right*) was an essential member of the Lewis and Clark expedition.

CHAPTER FIVE

*No woman accompanies
a war party.*

—Meriwether Lewis, 1805

OVERCOMING HARDSHIPS

The Shoshone bands lived on the Great Plains for centuries, roaming the lands and hunting bison and other large game. They adapted to their nomadic lifestyles and warred with other tribes to claim territory; however, they had not encountered other people apart from the tribes with which they fought. When horses arrived, their lives were improved; transportation became easier and hunting tactics quickly changed. Life would become much more complicated in the centuries to follow.

The first Europeans were explorers to a new territory, but soon settlers arrived and set up communities. Over the following decades, the Shoshone way of life would be transformed, their beliefs and customs threatened and challenged, and their perspective on the world altered in ways their ancestors could never have imagined.

Sacagawea

In 1803, Thomas Jefferson bought the Louisiana Territory from France. This added a large tract of land—828,000 square miles (2,144,510 square kilometers)—to the United States, doubling it in size. Jefferson quickly enlisted a group of men, led by Meriwether Lewis and William Clark, to travel to this new part of the country. His hope was for them to find a water route that connected the East Coast to the West Coast, as well as to map the area and record their findings.

In 1804, the group, called the Corps of Discovery, set off on their expedition. Along the way, the men kept detailed records of all they encountered—plants, animals, and people. These records still exist today and were used by explorers after them to guide them and identify their whereabouts.

The Shoshone bands lived in some of the territory acquired in the Louisiana Purchase. Some bands had already encountered French traders, but most had had little contact with Europeans.

Interestingly, the first Shoshone to meet the Lewis and Clark expedition was a woman, Sacagawea. Originally of the Lemhi band of Shoshone, for many years she had been held captive by a tribe called the Hidatsa in what is now North Dakota. After being

With the purchase of the Louisiana Territory, the United States became twice as large as it once was, opening up to many new opportunities and explorers such as Lewis and Clark.

sold to a French-Canadian trader named Toussaint Charbonneau, she stayed with him on a Hidatsa-Mandan settlement in North Dakota. Charbonneau had lived with the Mandan for many years, learning their language and accepting many of their traditions. Sacagawea learned both the Hidatsa and Shoshone languages. Sacagawea and Charbonneau would prove invaluable to the Lewis and Clark expedition as translators and negotiators.

The Corps of Discovery arrived at the Hidatsa-Mandan settlement on November 2, 1804. There, they soon met Charbonneau, who could converse with one of the expedition men, and Sacagawea, who could converse with the Native people. The corps quickly wished to enlist the service of these two on the remainder of their journey. However, Sacagawea was pregnant and could not travel with them until her child was born.

After Sacagawea had a baby boy in February 1805, the Corps of Discovery continued on their journey, along with Charbonneau, Sacagawea, and their child. The expedition traveled for months into new territory. Along the way, Sacagawea and her husband translated with Native groups and the expedition.

The Shoshone were great horse breeders, and their friendship was crucial for the expedition. On their journey, Lewis and Clark asked Sacagawea and her husband to secure horses for the group. Eventually, through negotiation and a chance meeting with Sacagawea's brother, the Shoshone provided horses, supplies, and guides to help the explorers on their journey to the Pacific Ocean. Warren Ferris, a fur trader, later recalled how the Shoshone had reacted to their encounter with Lewis and Clark: "Upon arriving at the strangers' encampment, they [the Shoshone] found, instead of an overwhelming force of their enemies, a few strangers like the two already with them, who treated them with great kindness, and gave them many things that had not existed before even in their dreams or imaginations." Yet the Shoshone were also "overwhelmed with fear, for we soon discovered that they were in possession of the identical thunder and lightning [firearms] that had proved in the hands of our foes so fatal to our happiness."

Sacagawea proved invaluable not only for her language skills but also for the mere fact that she was a woman. In many ways, the Corps of Discovery was more accepted because of Sacagawea's presence. A group consisting of all men could be seen as a threat, while if the group included a woman, especially one with a child, it was more likely to be considered approachable. Many Native groups agreed to work with the Corps of Discovery because Sacagawea was also part of their entourage.

Sacagawea and her family traveled all the way to the Pacific Ocean. On their voyage, she was instrumental to helping the expedition members survive. Her knowledge of plants, wildlife, and terrain allowed the group to avoid food poisoning, to heal injuries and illness, and to survive in rough weather.

After the expedition, Sacagawea and Charbonneau kept in contact with Clark, who became their son's godfather. Sadly, after the birth of her daughter in 1812, Sacagawea became very ill, possibly with typhoid fever. Some accounts of her life say she died that year, aged only twenty-five. Others claim she returned to her Native people and lived with them on the Wind River reservation, where she died in 1884. Mystery as to her true date of death remains to this day.

Despite the uncertainty of the latter part of her life, Sacagawea lives on as an immortal part of America's early history. Without her, the Corps of Discovery could have encountered many more difficulties, and the story of their journey could have ended in tragedy rather than triumph.

Following Lewis and Clark

Following the historic meeting with Lewis and Clark, the Shoshone maintained friendly relations with trappers and traders through the early 1800s. However, opportunities out West attracted more settlers and soldiers. Gold rushes and guarantees of land ownership

The Shoshone way of life changed with the arrival of settlers.

drew hundreds of people across the plains through the mid-1800s. These people challenged the Shoshone way of life. Many Shoshone and other Native bands became protective of their identity and their culture. Some bands went to war against the European "intruders," while others sought to live peacefully with them. The Northern Shoshone fought both settlers and soldiers, whom they viewed as invaders.

In a few short years, the Shoshone witnessed massive changes to the landscape and their everyday way of life. These changes were in the form of new modes of transportation, such as trains, a massive influx of settlers, and advances in communications technology—most importantly, the building of telegraph lines that could transport messages from one end of the country to the other. Through it all, the

Shoshone resisted these changes, wanting to uphold their traditional lifestyles.

Shoshone resistance to western expansion into and through their territory lasted just four years (1861–1865). While Union soldiers were occupied fighting the Civil War, Native Americans of the Great Basin, including the Shoshone, attacked wagon trains, **Pony Express** riders, and crews stringing telegraph lines.

To protect the travel routes, Patrick E. Connor formed the Third California Infantry of volunteers. In 1862, these troops established Fort Douglas in the foothills of the Wasatch Mountains, a range of the Rocky Mountains north of Salt Lake City. From this base, they patrolled areas of Nevada, Idaho, and Wyoming. In January 1863, Connor led three hundred volunteers north toward the village of Chief Bear Hunter whose Northern Shoshone had been attacking travelers through the region. The volunteers trudged 140 miles (225 km) through the fierce cold and deep snow to reach the village.

Bear Hunter's people had put up barricades of rocks and soil to better defend the village, which was situated in a ravine. However, the troops outflanked the Shoshone warriors, and on the morning of January 29, they devastated them with torrents of gunfire. In just four hours, as many as 250 Shoshone, including Bear Hunter, were slaughtered. Mormons who went to the site recalled, "the dead were eight feet deep [2.4 m] in one place." The volunteers destroyed more than seventy lodges and captured 175 horses, while only fourteen were killed and forty-nine were wounded among their own forces. Confronting the overwhelming military power of the soldiers, the Shoshone realized that they would have to make peace.

An End of an Era

In 1863, the Shoshone reluctantly signed the **Treaty** of Soda Springs, in which they agreed to adhere to certain boundaries and sell much of their land in exchange for money. However, this treaty was never ratified. By 1865, the US government had begun to force the Native Americans living there, including all the Shoshone, onto reservations. The Shoshone opposed relocation, but the Northern Shoshone were eventually made to move onto several reservations, including the Fort Hall Reservation in southeastern Idaho and the Duck Valley Reservation along the Nevada–Idaho border. The Western Shoshone were forced to relocate to the Western Shoshone Reservation on the border of Nevada and Idaho. The Gosiute (or Goshute), a branch of the Western Shoshone, were placed on the Goshute Reservation on the Nevada–Utah border and on the Skull Valley Reservation in western Utah. One band of mixed Shoshone and Bannock people known as the Mountain Sheep Eaters fought against removal until as late as 1878, when they too eventually relented and relocated. The Eastern Shoshone came to reside on the Wind River reservation in Wyoming.

Help from the Eastern Shoshone

Despite having been moved to a reservation in 1868, throughout the 1870s the Eastern Shoshone, led by a chief named Washakie, allied with the US Army in wars against the Sioux, Cheyenne, Arapaho, and Ute, mainly by serving as scouts in military campaigns. During the Sioux War of 1876, Washakie led a band of two hundred Shoshone, Bannock, and Ute warriors across the Rockies to fight alongside army troops under General George Crook. Although Washakie arrived too late to take part in the battle, he and his warriors helped pursue Crazy Horse and his Sioux followers.

Washakie and his people had been granted a large reservation in the Wind River valley of Wyoming. However, over the years, the size of the reservation was drastically reduced as later agreements were forced upon the Eastern Shoshone. In 1878, the Shoshone were compromised further when the Arapaho—their traditional enemies—were moved to Wind River to share the reservation with them. Washakie nonetheless advised that they continue friendly relations with the government. That year, President Ulysses S. Grant presented him with a saddle adorned with silver in recognition of his help over the years. In 1883, while on a fishing trip to Yellowstone National Park, President Chester Arthur visited Washakie. In 1897, after his son died in a senseless brawl, the great chief converted to Christianity. Three years later, he died at Flathead Village in the Bitterroot Valley of Montana and was buried in the Fort Washakie cemetery with full military honors. The inscription on his tombstone reads: "Always loyal to the Government and his white brothers."

Throughout his life, Washakie was famed not only for his skill and courage in battle, but for his friendship with pioneers and his loyalty to the US government. In the 1850s, when wagon trains had passed through Shoshone territory that bordered the Oregon Trail,

Washakie and his people had helped the overland travelers to ford streams and recover their cattle that had strayed away. He had ably served as a scout for the US Army and a trusted ally during the wars with the plains tribes. However, as he approached the end of his life, Washakie believed that he and his people had ultimately been betrayed by those whom they had so generously assisted. He voiced his outrage in the following statement:

The white man, who possesses this whole vast country from sea to sea, who roams over it at pleasure and lives where he likes, cannot know the cramp we feel in this little spot, with the underlying remembrance of the fact, which you know as well as we, that every foot of what you proudly call America not very long ago belonged to the red man. The Great Spirit gave it to us. There was room for all His many tribes, and all were happy in their freedom.

The white man's government promised that if we, the Shoshones, would be content with the little patch allowed us, it would keep us well supplied with everything necessary to comfortable living, and would see that no white man should cross our borders for our game or anything that is ours. But it has not kept its word! The white man kills our game, captures our furs, and sometimes feeds his herds upon our meadows. And your great and mighty government—oh sir, I hesitate, for I cannot tell the half! It does not protect our rights. It leaves us without the promised seed, without tools for cultivating the land, without implements for harvesting our crops, without breeding animals better than ours, without the food we still lack, after all we can do, without the many comforts we cannot produce, without the schools we so much need for our children.

I say again, the government does not keep its word!

Many Native people adopted this sentiment and held the government's actions against them for decades to follow. By 1900, the Native American way of life had irreversibly changed, many once thriving tribes having been forced thousands of miles from their ancestral lands.

Reservation Life

Life on the reservations proved hard for the Shoshone. After the death of Washakie in 1900, many Eastern Shoshone died of sickness and starvation. All the reservations lacked adequate food, clothing, shelter, and medicine. Having surrendered their land and abandoned their traditional way of life, the Shoshone found themselves impoverished and powerless. Most people had little hope for the future. In the 1930s, however, the New Deal under President Franklin Roosevelt brought self-government to Native peoples, including the Northern and Eastern Shoshone, in the form of the Tribal Council and the Business Council. Today, many of the reservations are self-governing, **sovereign** nations.

The Shoshone and Language

Shoshone belongs to a Central Numic group of the Uto-Aztecan language family. Central Numic includes three languages: Panamint, Shoshone, and Comanche. Within Shoshone there are three regional variations, or dialects, called Northern, Eastern, and Western. Since the differences are slight, any one of these dialects can be understood by all Shoshone people.

The following examples are based primarily on material provided in *Newe Natekwinappeh: Shoshoni Stories and Dictionary*, compiled by Wick R. Miller. Shoshone is a complicated language, but the following key and examples should be helpful for the basic pronunciation of words.

Vowels are generally pronounced as follows:

a	as in father
e	as in pan
i	as in tin
o	as in go
u	as in put

In some cases, vowels are written twice, as in *aa*. These vowels are stressed somewhat more than single vowels. When vowels occur together, as in *ia* and *ea*, they usually have the same sounds as when spoken separately. However, *ai* is pronounced either as the *i* in bite or the e in bet. In the latter case, the *ai* is underlined.

The consonants are generally pronounced as in English, except for the glottal stop, a catch in the throat, as in the slight pause between the two syllables when the word "uh oh!" is spoken. A glottal stop is indicated by a '.

Here are some everyday words used by the Shoshone:

Sayings

pehnaho	hello
kai	no
maikkuh, tsumaikku	OK
haa	yes

Relatives

paha, tokka	aunt
tuine, natuipittsi, piia	boy
papi	brother (older)
tami	brother (younger)
appe	father
haintseh, te'I	friend
nai-pin	girl
tainkwa, tsuku, tuittsi	man
pia, pii	mother
patsi	sister (older)
nammi	sister (younger)
ata, hai, tsukuhnaa	uncle
wa'ippe	woman

Parts of the Body

peta	arm
nenkappeh, yenka-ppeh	chest

nainkih	ear
kii-ppeh	elbow
puih	eye
kopai	face
maseki	finger
nampai	foot
mo'o	hand
pam-pin	head
pihyen	heart
tanka-ppeh	knee
oon	leg
tempai	mouth
mu-pin, muitsun	nose
tsoa-ppeh	shoulder
taseki	toe

Nature

pakena-ppeh	cloud
soko-ppeh	earth
mea	moon
toya-pin	mountain
tukum-pin	sky
takka	snow
tapai	sun
soho-pin	tree
yakun	valley
paa	water

The People and Culture of the Shoshone

Animals

kwahaten, wantsi	antelope
weeta, akoai	bear
kwinaa, huittsuu	bird
kuittsun	buffalo
itsa-ppe	coyote
teheyan	deer
satii	dog
peyan	duck
kwinaa	eagle
noyo	egg
pateheyan	elk
painkwi, akai	fish
waako	frog
punku	horse
tapun	rabbit, cottontail
kammu	rabbit, jack
tokoa	rattlesnake
akai	salmon
tukku	sheep, mountain

Like all Native communities, the Shoshone remember their ancestors in many ways: preserving the language has become an important facet of passing on their history to future generations.

Today, the younger generation of Shoshone has adopted many modern pastimes.

CHAPTER SIX

Song Woman
Sits beating the rhythm
of her song.

—Western Shoshone
song

THE NATION'S PRESENCE NOW

Today, the Shoshone continue their traditions and celebrations on eighteen reservations throughout the western United States. These reservations are located in Utah, Nevada, Idaho, and California. Some reservations are shared with other Native tribes, such as the Arapaho, Bannock, and Paiute. Others are sovereign nations operated by the Shoshone band alone.

Horses remain important to the Shoshone way of life.

Growing Numbers

In the nineteenth century, there were about three thousand Northern Shoshone, two thousand Western Shoshone, and two thousand Eastern Shoshone. Today, it is estimated that more than 41,000 people in the United States are descendants of the four original Shoshone tribes.

Many Shoshone members live on or near the many reservations. Reservation life is not always easy, however. Many people struggle with issues such as unemployment and alcoholism. On some reservations, the Shoshone

have benefited from business enterprises, such as
cattle ranching, while others have been engaged in
legal battles to reclaim their lands and their rights.
The Shoshone continue to uphold their beliefs and
traditions despite hardships faced. In many communities,
improvements are being made to ensure the survival and
success of the Shoshone people.

The Northern Shoshone

Today many bands of Northern Shoshone live on the
Fort Hall Reservation in Idaho, along with the Bannock
tribe. Together, they form the Shoshone-Bannock
Tribes. As of August 2015, the number of Native
people from both bands living on the reservation
totaled 4,038. Together, the Shoshone-Bannock Tribes
have formed a community on the Snake River Plain. The
two tribes have long lived together, and their histories
have become intertwined through the centuries.

Every year, the Shoshone-Bannock Tribes on the Fort
Hall Reservation celebrate by holding the Shoshone-
Bannock Indian Festival, one of the largest powwows in
North America. Top powwow dancers and drum groups
from across the United States and Canada come to Fort
Hall every August to take part in the festivities, which
include a rodeo, relay races, and parades. Established
by presidential executive order in 1867 and confirmed
by the terms of the Fort Bridger Treaty of 1868, the
reservation originally comprised 1.8 million acres
(728 ha), but was reduced to 1.2 million acres (486 ha)
in 1872 by a surveying error. Over the years, further
encroachments reduced the reservation to its present
size. Today, the tribes on the Fort Hall Reservation are

Each year, the Shoshone celebrate with dances, songs, and ceremonies.

The People and Culture of the Shoshone

organized as their own sovereign government, which provides many resources for tribal members, including education, health, and social services. Tribal leaders also manage agriculture, business enterprises, tourism, and other revenue-generating operations for the reservation.

There are many opportunities for economic growth on the reservation. Fort Hall has many businesses, such as gas stations and fish hatcheries. Likewise, since 1966, the Shoshone-Bannock Tribes have run their own bison herd. Today, the number of bison on the reservation is between three hundred and four hundred. This brings in revenue by providing meat and furs to nearby communities and around the world. One of the newer activities added to the reservation is the Sage Hill Travel Center and Casino. It was built in 2009 and has attracted many visitors since it opened. However, despite such successes, hardships remain. For example, the unemployment rate on the reservation is around 18 percent. Many members also struggle with addictions and alcoholism. Similar trends are seen on other Shoshone reservations. Likewise, there was a push in the early twenty-first century to gain lost ancestral lands for the Lemhi Shoshone who, having been moved from the Lemhi Valley Indian Reservation in the early 1900s, came to live at Fort Hall Reservation.

Not all of the Northern Shoshone live at the Fort Hall Reservation, however. Members of the Northwestern Band of Shoshone—a federally recognized branch of Shoshone as of April 29, 1987— live in the areas surrounding the reservation or in other parts of the United States, especially southern Idaho and northern Utah. They work as doctors, lawyers, politicians, teachers, and civil servants.

The Eastern Shoshone

Many Eastern Shoshone live on the Wind River Reservation in Lander, Wyoming. At over 2.2 million acres (8.9 million ha), it is the seventh-largest reservation in the United States. It is home to both the Eastern Shoshone and the Northern Arapaho tribes. As of 2015, there were 3,909 members enrolled in the tribe. Originally rivals, these two tribes have learned to work together as one community over the decades since the reservation was established. Each year, the reservation hosts powwows. Primarily in the summer, these events showcase special dances and customs from both Native tribes. Many people participate in

Traditions such as cow roping are continued at ceremonies such as Indian Days at the Wind River Reservation.

these events, or come to watch the festivities and witness firsthand two cultures in action.

If members of the community around the reservation want to learn even more, the Wind River Reservation includes several museums that feature exhibits about the land, the people, and the area's history.

Many Shoshone people today work in fields such as environmental conservation, engineering, and surveying.

The Western Shoshone

When forced onto reservation lands in the 1860s, some Western Shoshone eluded authorities. This lasted until the 1930s, when, as an alternative, the US government allowed scattered groups to settle in small colonies (known as ranches or rancherías) in California. Many of these rancherías still exist today. Four groups of Western Shoshone have banded together to form the Te-Moak Tribe of Western Shoshone with headquarters in Elko, Nevada. The Western Shoshone gained recognition as a tribe by the federal government in 1982. Other reservations on which Western Shoshone live are the Confederated Tribes of Goshute Reservation on the Nevada–Utah border, the Skull Valley Reservation in Utah, and the Duck Valley Indian Reservation in Idaho. As of 2009, less than seven hundred Goshute people remained. Altogether, tribal enrollment of the Western Shoshone is estimated at around ten thousand.

The Western Shoshone assert that they never surrendered their land in the Treaty of Ruby Valley in 1863. They have long sought claims against the US government. In 1984, several tribal members established the Western Shoshone National Council to handle these land claims. Instead of accepting financial compensation, this organization attempted to reclaim portions of the estimated 22 million acres (89 million ha) of Shoshone territory seized by the federal government in the nineteenth century. In the early 2000s, the Western Shoshone were also engaged in a bitter dispute with the Bureau of Land Management over grazing rights in Nevada. Today, the Western Shoshone continue to strive for more land, and issues of grazing rights reappeared in 2014.

The members of the Western Shoshone living on the Duck Valley Reservation share it with members of the Northern Paiute tribe. Every year, the two tribes celebrate their cultures with numerous powwows and other cultural events.

A Shoshone brother and sister collect sunflowers at the Fort Hall Reservation in Idaho.

Ensuring Survival

While adapting to a modern way of life, the Shoshone have also worked to preserve their language and traditions throughout the Great Basin. Like Coyote, they continue to be skillful and clever survivors. Wherever they make their home, the Shoshone are both embracing technological innovations and striving to maintain their artistic traditions, language, and heritage for themselves and future generations.

Many of the Shoshone communities have created a presence online, usually through websites but also through tribal Facebook and Twitter accounts, as well as YouTube channels. These outlets allow the tribes to extend their experiences and knowledge to people all around the world. By doing so, they ensure their communities, history, and beliefs continue for many decades to come.

Chief Garfield Pocatello,
March 1913.

CHAPTER SEVEN

Despite hardship, the Shoshone people endure today.

FACES OF THE SHOSHONE

Throughout history, the Shoshone have produced many well-known members. Some of these men and women have left indelible marks on the history of the Shoshone as well as on the history of the United States. Here are some of the most famous Shoshone from over the centuries:

Bear Hunter (died 1863), also known as Wirasuap or Bear Spirit, lived in a village along the Bear River that flows into the Great Salt Lake in Utah. During the early 1860s, Native Americans in the Great Basin, including Bear Hunter, often made raids against the miners and Mormons. They also attacked wagon trains and stagecoaches on the Central Overland Route to California, as well as Pony Express riders and crews putting up telegraph lines.

Because US troops were involved with the Civil War, they were not available to protect settlers and travelers in the West. To keep the routes open, the Third California Infantry of volunteers was organized under Patrick E. Connor. In 1862, these troops established Fort Douglas in the foothills of the Wasatch Mountains, a range of the Rocky Mountains overlooking Salt Lake City. From this base, they patrolled areas of Nevada, Idaho, and Wyoming. In January 1863, Connor led a force of three hundred troops northward toward Bear Hunter's village. The men trudged 140 miles (225 km) through bitter cold and deep snow to devastate the village with gunfire. In the fighting that lasted four hours, as many as 250 Shoshone, including Bear Hunter, were killed. The Shoshone were later forced to sign a treaty in which much of the Great Basin was taken from them.

Jean Baptiste Charbonneau (1805–1866), son of Sacagawea and Toussaint Charbonneau, was born during the Lewis and Clark encampment among the Hidatsa-Mandan people. During the journey to the Pacific Ocean and the return trip, Sacagawea carried the baby, also called Pomp, Pompy, or Pompey, on her back in a cradleboard. In some versions of his life, William Clark was asked to care for the boy sometime after 1806, and he eventually sent the child to a Catholic school.

Many years later, in 1823, Charbonneau was persuaded by Prince Paul Wilhelm of Germany to journey with him to Europe. He spent the next six years there, traveling and studying languages. Charbonneau returned to America with Prince Paul in 1829, and the two men explored the upper reaches of the Missouri River. Charbonneau became a fur trapper in an area of the Rocky Mountains that is now Utah and Idaho. He befriended several mountain men, including the legendary James Bridger, and joined in a trappers' rendezvous on the Green River in 1833.

When the fur trade declined in the 1830s, Charbonneau became a guide for explorers along the upper Missouri River. Along with Louis Vasquez and Andrew Sublette, he helped establish Fort Vasquez on the South Platte River near present-day Denver, Colorado, in 1839–1840. He explored the Yellowstone region with Scottish nobleman William Drummond in 1843. He also worked as a guide for the US Corps of Topographical Engineers in 1845. A year later, during the Mexican-American War (1846–1848), he served as a guide for federal soldiers traveling from Santa Fe, New Mexico, to San Diego, California. After the war, he remained in California to prospect for gold. In 1866, while on his way to gold strikes in Montana, he died somewhere along the Owyhee River near the border of Oregon, Idaho, and Montana.

Pocatello (circa 1815–1884), head chief of the Shoshone living in the Grouse Creek region, became leader in 1847—the same year that the Mormons arrived in Salt Lake City. As settlers and miners poured through the region, Native Americans made frequent raids for which Pocatello's band was often blamed. In later years, especially after he was briefly imprisoned in 1859, the great chief tried to maintain neutrality with the Mormons, miners, and other Native Americans in the region. In January 1863, he left Bear Hunter's village the day before the attack by Patrick E. Connor and his California volunteers. In July of that same year, he negotiated with Governor James Doty and signed a peace treaty. From 1867 to 1869, he took part in bison hunts with Washakie's Wind River Shoshone and the Bannock.

In 1869, the Union Pacific and Central Pacific railroads joined at Promontory Point, Utah. With the completion of the transcontinental railroad, more settlers poured into the region. By the end of 1872, Pocatello and his people, the Northwestern band of Shoshones, were forced to settle on the Fort Hall Reservation in southeastern Idaho. Pocatello converted to Mormonism to live at the farm of the missionary George Hill on the lower Bear River near Corrine, Utah. However, people in the town demanded that the converts, including Pocatello, be returned to the reservation. Rejecting Mormonism, Pocatello lived the rest of his life on the reservation. A nearby city in Idaho is named for him.

Sacagawea is commemorated on buildings, coins, and statues around the United States.

Sacagawea (ca. 1784–ca. 1812 or 1884), or Bird Woman, the Native guide and interpreter for the Lewis and Clark expedition, was born to the Lemhi Shoshone, who lived in what is now central Idaho and western Montana. When she was a teenager, Sacagawea was taken captive by the Hidatsa and brought to their village on the upper Missouri River in present-day North Dakota. In 1804, she was either purchased or won in a wager by a French-Canadian trader named Toussaint Charbonneau. In May of that year, Lewis and Clark began their journey up the Missouri River from St. Louis. They wintered with the Mandan and met Charbonneau, who they hired as an interpreter. The trader insisted that Sacagawea, who spoke Shoshone and who wished to rejoin her people, be allowed to travel with them.

In February of 1805—less than two months before the explorers left Fort Mandan in April—Sacagawea gave birth to Charbonneau's son, Jean Baptiste, who was nicknamed Pomp during the expedition. With a cradleboard on her back, Sacagawea played a major role in the success of the journey. She guided the explorers through the wilderness and helped sustain them with wild plants. Through sign language, she was able to communicate with all the Native peoples encountered during the journey. She even served as a peacemaker with hostile Native tribes.

In August, at the Three Forks of the Missouri River in what is now Montana, she was finally reunited with her brother, Cameahwait. At Sacagawea's request, Cameahwait, who was now chief of his band, provided horses, supplies, and guides to help the expedition cross the Rocky Mountains. In November 1805, the expedition reached the Pacific Ocean. On the return trip, Sacagawea traveled with Clark's party along the Yellowstone River. She and Charbonneau left the expedition at the Hidatsa village on the Knife River, while Lewis and Clark returned to St. Louis in 1806.

No one knows when or where Sacagawea died, and the accounts vary dramatically. In one version, she and Charbonneau came to St. Louis after 1806 and left their son with Clark to be educated. With trader Manuel Lisa, the couple then journeyed back up the Missouri River, where Sacagawea died from an unknown disease in 1812. In another account, Sacagawea lived with the Comanches, then returned to her homeland and lived at Washakie's Wind River Reservation in Wyoming until her death at the age of eighty or older.

Sacagawea has been honored in many history books and memorials, including a minted gold-colored coin in 2000. A river, mountain, and pass are also named for her.

Tendoy (Tendoi) (ca. 1834–1907), principal chief of the Lemhis, was born near the Boise River in Idaho. The son of a Bannock war chief and a Shoshone woman, Tendoy became the leader of a band of Bannock and Shoshone who made their home in the Lemhi Valley of Idaho. The band lived by fishing in the Lemhi and Salmon Rivers and bison hunting in western Montana. However, when gold prospectors flooded into the region in the 1860s, they so disrupted the traditional ways of hunting and gathering that Tendoy's people faced starvation.

Tendoy worked to maintain peaceful relations with the men in the Montana mining camps as he made trading journeys to provide for his band. In 1868, the federal government established the Fort Hall Reservation in southeastern Idaho, but Tendoy and his people remained in the Lemhi Valley to the north. Like the Wind River Band of Eastern Shoshones under the leadership of Washakie, Tendoy remained peaceful through many conflicts in the region. These included raids by Pocatello and Bear Hunter in the 1850s and 1860s, the Paiute War of 1860, the Nez Perce War in 1877, and the Bannock War of 1878.

In 1875, President Ulysses S. Grant issued an executive order allowing Tendoy and his people to remain on their ancestral lands. However, in 1892, Tendoy was forced to sign a treaty with the government and finally settled on the Fort Hall Reservation. The editor of the *Idaho Recorder* newspaper of Salmon

Chief Tendoy (*right*) is pictured here at Fort Hall Reservation.

City wrote of the removal, "Now the crowning sorrow is forced upon this good chief and his long-suffering band. They are being forced from the land of their birth, from the beautiful Lemhi valley, to a distant reservation to make homes among people whom they

The People and Culture of the Shoshone

fear and dislike to the extreme of hate. The heart of the good Tendoy is broken by this last act of ingratitude." Tendoy's descendants live on the Fort Hall Reservation.

Washakie (ca.1804–1900), principal chief of the Eastern Shoshone, was also known as Gourd Rattle. He spent his early years in the Bitterroot Mountains in what is now Montana with the Flathead tribe of his father. After his father's death, Washakie and his Shoshone mother went to live with her people in the Wind River Mountains, a range of the Rockies in what is now western Wyoming. As a young man, Washakie became renowned as a warrior in raids against the Blackfeet and Crow.

Like the Lemhi Shoshone under the leadership of Tendoy, the Wind River Shoshone (also known as the Eastern Shoshone), maintained peaceful relations with trappers and traders. During the 1820s and 1830s, Washakie became friends with Kit Carson, James Bridger, and other mountain men. Washakie hunted and trapped animals for pelts that he traded for guns, tools, and cloth. He also encouraged his people to trade furs for goods. By the late 1840s, Washakie had become the principal chief of his band. He remained friendly with the settlers making their way along the Oregon Trail and even ordered groups of warriors to patrol the region and help travelers to ford rivers and find lost livestock. He became friends with the Mormons and spent part of one winter in the home of their leader, Brigham Young.

During the campaign against Bear Hunter's band in January 1863, Washakie led his people to safety at

Chief Washakie

The People and Culture of the Shoshone

Fort Bridger. In July 1863, he signed a treaty allowing settlers for twenty years to travel peacefully through his territory in exchange for payments. In July 1868, he signed another treaty granting a right-of-way to the Union Pacific Railroad and agreeing to settle on a reservation. After federal troops had established Camp Brown at what is now Lander, Wyoming, Washakie and other men in his band served as scouts in army campaigns against the Sioux, Cheyenne, Arapaho, and Ute.

In 1878, Camp Brown, which had been moved to the north and south forks of the Little Wind River, was renamed Fort Washakie. The same year—despite Washakie's protests—the Arapaho were moved to the Wind River Reservation with the Shoshone. In 1883, President Chester Arthur, who was on a fishing trip to Yellowstone National Park, visited Washakie. When his son died in a bar fight in 1897, Washakie converted to Christianity. He died three years later at Flathead Village in the Bitterroot Valley of Montana. He was buried in the Fort Washakie cemetery with full military honors.

Many other men and women have come after these historical figures, and through it all, they have continued the presence of the Shoshone bands. By keeping the history of these people alive, the Shoshone will continue to be a lasting presence in the world and in Native American heritage.

CHRONOLOGY

before 1000 The ancestors of the Shoshone make their way into the Great Basin.

circa 1700 The Shoshone and other Native Americans east of the Rocky Mountains acquire horses.

1782 The Eastern Shoshone are devastated by a smallpox epidemic and attacks by the Blackfeet.

ca. 1788 Sacagawea is born in northern Shoshone territory in what is now Idaho.

1803 President Thomas Jefferson acquires from France for $15 million a vast tract of land west of the Mississippi River known as the Louisiana Purchase.

1804–1805 The Lewis and Clark expedition explores the American West. The group eventually reaches the Pacific Ocean with the help of the Shoshone and Sacagawea as a guide.

1847 Mormons settle in Shoshone territory in the Salt Lake Valley of Utah.

1848 In the Treaty of Guadalupe Hidalgo, Mexico cedes a large tract of land, including Shoshone territory, to the United States. Gold is discovered in California.

1859 Settlers pour into Nevada when gold and silver mines open at the Comstock Lode.

1863 The Shoshone are defeated in the Battle of Bear River, also known as the Bear River Massacre or the Bannock Wars.

1869 President Ulysses S. Grant introduces policies to extinguish Native American traditions and religions.

1900 Chief Washakie dies.

1934 The Indian Reorganization Act grants Native Americans greater control of their tribal affairs.

1972 The Indian Self-Determination Act grants tribes more control over local laws and greater involvement in government policy.

1982 The Western Shoshone are recognized as a tribe by the federal government.

1984 The Western Shoshone National Council is formed to handle tribal land claims.

1985 The Northwestern Band of Shoshone becomes a federally recognized tribe.

1988 The Wind River Shoshone form a task force to study living conditions on their reservation.

1991 To stimulate economic growth, the Northern Shoshone open gambling operations on their reservation.

2000 The US Mint commemorates Sacagawea with a gold $1 coin.

2004 The United States celebrates the 200th anniversary of the Lewis and Clark expedition.

2009 The Northern Shoshone open Sage Hill Travel Center and Casino.

2014 The Western Shoshone again argue for land grazing rights.

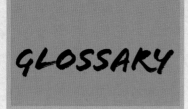

GLOSSARY

Appe Meaning "father," name given the sun, revered by the Western Shoshone as the creator of heaven and earth.

Bannock A Northern Paiute group that moved from Oregon into Idaho and lived with the Northern Shoshone; Bannock people today share Fort Hall Reservation with the Shoshone.

Bering Strait The body of water that separates Russia and Alaska. During the last Ice Age, a land bridge across the strait allowed for migration from one continent to the other.

camas A kind of lily whose bulbs were dug and eaten by the Shoshone and other Native peoples.

counting coup Touching an enemy in battle to prove one's bravery.

Great Basin An arid region that includes Utah, Nevada, and parts of the adjoining states.

Great Plains A vast area of flat or gently rolling grasslands between the Mississippi River and the Rocky Mountains.

Louisiana Purchase A tract of land bought by the United States from France in 1803 comprising the territory west of the Mississippi River.

moccasins Soft leather shoes often decorated with brightly colored beads.

Numic A branch of the Uto-Aztecan language family that includes Shoshone, Ute, and other languages of the Great Basin.

parfleche A leather pouch for storing food, clothing, and other belongings.

pemmican Dried, pounded meat mixed with fat and berries, used as energy food by warriors on long journeys.

piñon A small pine tree of the American Southwest that bears seeds collected and eaten by the Shoshone and other Native people.

Pony Express A way of quickly delivering mail using a horse and mailman carrying bags of correspondence.

reservation A tract of land set aside for Native Americans.

sovereign Independent; able to make its own decisions.

sweat lodge A dome-shaped hut of sticks covered with bison skins or mud in which purifications and other sacred ceremonies are held.

taboo A strict prohibition, something that is forbidden.

tipi A portable, cone-shaped home made of poles covered with animal skins.

travois A sled made of two poles lashed together and pulled by a dog or horse.

treaty A signed, legal agreement between two nations.

tribal council The legal governing body for each Shoshone reservation.

vision quest A ritual in which a person fasts and prays alone in hopes of receiving a vision from the spirits.

weir A trap placed across a stream or river to catch fish.

BIBLIOGRAPHY

Collins, Terry. *Into the West: Causes and Effects of US Westward Expansion*. North Mankato, MN: Capstone Press, 2013.

Del Monte, H. D. *Life of Chief Washakie and Shoshone Indians*. Whitefish, MT: Literary Licensing, 2011.

DeVoto, Bernard, ed. *The Journals of Lewis and Clark*. Umpqua, OR: River Canyon Press, 2010. Kindle edition.

Jager, Rebecca K. *Malinche, Pocahontas, and Sacagawea: Indian Women as Cultural Intermediaries and National Symbols*. Norman, OK: University of Oklahoma Press, 2015.

Jazynka, Kitson. *Sacagawea*. National Geographic Kids. Washington, DC: National Geographic, 2015.

Josephy, Alvin Jr. *Lewis and Clark Through Indian Eyes: Nine Indian Writers on the Legacy of the Expedition*. New York: Random House, 2007.

Meacham, Jon. *Thomas Jefferson: The Art of Power*. New York: Random House, 2013.

Northwestern Band of the Shoshone Nation. *Coyote Steals Fire: A Shoshone Tale*. Logan, UT: Utah State University Press, 2005.

Raum, Elizabeth. *Expanding a Nation: Causes and Effects of the Louisiana Purchase*. North Mankato, MN: Capstone, 2013.

Stamm, Henry E., IV *People of the Wind River: Eastern Shoshones 1825–1900*. Norman, OK: University of Oklahoma Press, 1999.

FURTHER INFORMATION

Want to know more about the Shoshone? Check out these websites, videos, and organizations.

Websites

History: Sacagawea

www.history.com/topics/native-american-history/Sacagawea

Learn more about the life and adventures of Sacagawea.

National Geographic: Lewis and Clark Expedition

www.nationalgeographic.com/lewisandclark

This interactive website explores the world of Lewis and Clark and follows them on their journey across the West.

Northwestern Band of the Shoshone Nation

www.nwbshoshone.com

This website discusses the history and culture of the Northwestern Band of Shoshone.

Shoshone-Bannock Festival

www.sbtribes.com/festival

Enjoy this slideshow from the 52nd Annual Shoshone-Bannock Festival.

Shoshone-Bannock Tribal Website

www.shoshonebannocktribes.com

This website provides a wealth of information about the reservation and the tribes' activities, including current events.

Videos

Eastern Shoshone Powwow 2013

www.youtube.com/watch?v=LiETWJForyE

This video shows footage from the 2013 Eastern Shoshone Powwow, complete with formal processionals, dances, and music.

Shoshone-Paiute History

www.youtube.com/watch?v=AnTaYEsXWAk

This video explores the history of the Shoshone-Paiute tribes.

Westward Strategy: The Louisiana Purchase and the Lewis and Clark Expedition

www.youtube.com/watch?v=s-ngy5k-7yg

This video teaches about the Louisiana Purchase and Lewis and Clark's adventure across the West.

Organizations

Battle Mountain Shoshone

37 Mountain View Drive

Battle Mountain, NV 89820

(775) 635-2004

www.temoaktribe.com/battlemtn.shtml

Ely Shoshone

16 Shoshone Circle

Ely, NV 89301

(775) 289-3013

Fort McDermitt Shoshone-Paiute

PO Box 457

McDermitt, NV 89421

(775) 532-8259

Northwestern Band of Shoshone

707 N Main St

Brigham City, UT

(208) 478-5712

www.nwbshoshone.com

Shoshone-Bannock Tribes

PO Box 306

Fort Hall, ID 83203

(208) 478-3700

www.shoshonebannocktribes.com

Shoshone-Piaute
PO Box 219
Owyhee, NV 89832
(208) 759-3100

South Park Shoshone
PO Box B-13
Lee, NV 89829
(702) 744-4273

Te-Moak Shoshone
525 Sunset Street
Elko, NV 89801
(775) 738-9251

Timba-Sha (Timbisha) Western Shoshone
(Death Valley Indian Community)
621 West Line St. #109
Bishop, CA 93514
(760) 872-3614
timbisha.com

Wind River Reservation
PO Box 925
Lander, WY 82520
(800) 645-6233
www.windriver.org

Wells Shoshone
PO Box 809
Wells, NV 89835
(775) 752-3045
www.temoaktribe.com/wells.shtml

Yomba Shoshone
HC 61 Box 6275
Austin, NV 89310
(775) 964-2463
www.yombatribe.org

INDEX

Page numbers in **boldface** are illustrations. Entries in **boldface** are glossary terms.

ABOUT THE AUTHORS

Cassie M. Lawton is a freelance editor and writer living and working in New York City.

Raymond Bial has published more than eighty books—most of them photography books—during his career. His photo-essays for children include *Corn Belt Harvest, Amish Home, Frontier Home, Shaker Home, The Underground Railroad, Portrait of a Farm Family, With Needle and Thread: A Book About Quilts, Mist Over the Mountains: Appalachia and Its People, Cajun Home,* and *Where Lincoln Walked.*

As with his other work, Bial's deep feeling for his subjects is evident in both the text and illustrations. He travels to tribal cultural centers, photographing homes, artifacts, and surroundings and learning firsthand about the national lifeways of these peoples.

The emeritus director of a small college library in the Midwest, he lives with his wife and three children in Urbana, Illinois.